MW00345920

BLUE & WHITE
STYLE

BLUE & WHITE STYLE

classic and contemporary
interiors, from mediterranean
to country blue

GAIL ABBOTT

PHOTOGRAPHY MARK SCOTT

CICO BOOKS

LONDON NEW YORK

For my father, Ralph Cooper

1924–2007

This edition published in 2015 by CICO Books
an imprint of Ryland Peters & Small
20–21 Jockey's Fields   341 E 116th St
London WC1R 4BW   New York, NY 10029

10 9 8 7 6 5 4 3 2 1

First published in 2008 by CICO Books as *Decorating with Blue and White*

A CIP catalog record for this book is available from the Library of Congress and the British Library.

ISBN: 978 1 78249 189 7

Printed in China

Editor: Gillian Haslam
Designer: Christine Wood
Photographer: Mark Scott

Art director: Sally Powell
Production manager: Gordana Simankovic
Publishing manager: Penny Craig
Publisher: Cindy Richards

contents

introduction

Of all the combinations of color, blue and white seems to be the most perennial, a favorite throughout the ages for craftsmen, artists, and decorators alike. The two together always remind us of nature at its most beautiful—or at its most dramatic. From the tranquil cerulean of a tropical sea lapping a beach of white sand to an exhilarating bank of white-tipped clouds highlighted against a storm-laden sky, blue and white always lifts the spirits. Nature in all its forms uses blue and white with a far-reaching liberality. Think of the brilliance in the heart of a sapphire, a shimmering haze of bluebells in spring, or the glowing petals of an iris.

Because of its strong links with nature, blue is a universal color, surely loved in one of its forms by everyone; white reminds us of purity and innocence and contains all other colors within it, and both have a seemingly infinite range of tones and hues. If pure blue veers toward the greens that lie next to it in the spectrum, it becomes aquamarine, cerulean, and turquoise—cool, clear watery hues that have associations with lakes, oceans, and rivers. When tinged with purple, blue assumes the warmth seen in royal blue, indigo, and navy—colors that make us feel confident and safe.

When it's mixed with white to create a range of gentle pastel shades, blue becomes pale and airy, with tints that convey a feeling of relaxed space and the far-distant horizons. If tinged with black, it assumes a more substantial air, redolent of the gray clouds and overcast skies found in the Northern hemisphere.

And white is not just white. It can be as fresh and brilliant as a field of snow reflecting the blue sky, as creamy as a bowl of Jersey milk, or as softly gray as the feathers on a dove's breast.

right: Soft sky blue and white is a classic combination, and in a white open-plan room where checks and stripes provide the only decorative pattern, the small space looks airy and spacious. The colors are an exact reflection of the sea and sky just outside the door.

below: Because blue is such a universal colour, don't worry about matching the different tones perfectly. Warm hues and cool shades sit together easily without clashing, and plenty of white helps them to harmonize.

below right: Be inspired by nature's colors and use postcards, magazines, and your own holiday photographs to take note of the way many different blues can be used together. The vivid hues of the sea are always sure to give you ideas.

Decorating with blue and white can mean starting from scratch and transforming a whole room using wallpaper to achieve a new look, or it might suggest painting the outside of an old display cabinet with white, and then giving it a surprising interior of pure blue. It could be as simple as piling a clutch of mismatched cushions and pillows on the sofa for instant effect, finding a new set of blue-and-white china for tea in the garden, or re-covering a favorite armchair in blue-and-white gingham. A love of blue and white might persuade you to search for vintage enameled storage jars in your local junk store, or start a collection of antique patterned plates. Once you get started, there's no knowing where it might lead you.

The ideas in this book have been taken from houses as different as a white beach house near Cape Town, an ancient farmhouse on the south coast of England, a restored riad in Marrakech, and an American-style white clapboard cottage—all very diverse homes with their own histories. But the joy of using a blue and white theme is that it can be applied to give an infinite number of effects wherever it is used, from crisply contemporary and stylishly chic to delicately faded and muted, from relaxed country to traditionally classic.

Use the wealth of inspiration that you can see all around you in nature and combine it with the ideas found here. However you decide to combine the two, this is a look that's easy to get right.

below: Blue woodwork and white walls are a classic combination that will give any room an understated country feel, especially if the blue chosen is a soft, green-blue and the white has undertones of gray or cream.

below right: Use blue accessories in a room with a neutral wall color and white furniture and your blue-and-white scheme will slot into place effortlessly. Valance, quilt, and bed linen are the underlying elements here, but a pair of denim pillows gives the blues particular emphasis.

left: Classic elements make up a faded yet elegant sitting room. The armchairs and footstool are traditionally shaped, but all are upholstered in crisp white linen with blue-and-white cushions. The distressed, white-painted mantelpiece displays a collection of new and old blue pieces.

right: It would be hard to find any civilization throughout history that has not cherished flowers, and as society became more industrialized, floral printed fabrics, like this classic blue floral design, grew in popularity.

classic blues

The use of blue and white for interior decoration has been popular since ancient times, and blue and white have been discovered together on wall and ceiling mosaics in villas excavated in Pompeii, which date back to the first century AD. In fact, the Romans used the rare blue of the indigo plant, found in India, to dye their furnishing fabrics. It is no coincidence that combinations of blue and white so often appeared in early civilizations, especially those around the shores of the Mediterranean, with its vivid cerulean skies and azure seas.

making an entrance

The modern preference for natural wood floors and striped stair runners has been heralded by our love for the pale, natural-looking interiors influenced by Scandinavian style. In Sweden, hand-woven rugs using pastel stripes, and made with woven strips of rags, are often handed down from mother to daughter and there is a long tradition of narrow runners which are used to soften the bareness of a pale wooden floor. Practical and hard wearing, a wood or wood-look floor—whether real wood, veneer, or laminated—is easy to maintain and easier to clean than a fitted carpet, especially in a hallway that gets a lot of wear.

In the nineteenth and earlier part of the twentieth centuries, it was customary to treat the edges of stairs and the banisters with a dark brown varnish, and to fit a long runner in the center of the stairs, making ill-lit halls and stairs dark and gloomy places. The tradition of fitting a stair runner has found a new place in modern interiors, especially in hallways of Victorian houses built over a century ago. With walls and woodwork as well as the edges of the stairs painted in a reflective white and with the addition of a colorful flat-weave runner, an originally unprepossessing entrance hall can be made to look bright and light, greeting family and friends alike with a cheerful welcome.

above: An original Victorian door still has its beautiful stained glass edges. The corner stars in blue and white are a design classic, and influenced the choice of color for the stair runner.

left: Contemporary steel grippers make it unnecessary to use stair rods to hold runners in place, but it is a classic touch that anchors the style in its tradition. It's best to seek out a qualified tradesman to fit flat-weave carpets, especially if there are curving stairs to be fitted.

left: This block-printed wallpaper is printed with the most environmentally-friendly water-based paints using traditional methods. The design is taken from a pattern found at Uppark, an eighteenth-century English country house.

right: The contrast between the soft blue and white of the wallpaper and the black of the cast-iron lantern is startling, but it's a disparity that adds drama and excitement to a normally unnoticed area.

heavenly blues

In the great houses and palaces in eighteenth-century Europe, elaborately painted blue-and-white ceilings were an accepted part of interior decoration. Blue skies with white clouds were peopled with angelic cherubs and "putti" resembling small, fat babies, as well as being crowded with saints and allegorical characters. A contemporary version is achieved here in an English farmhouse by papering the ceiling with a classically-styled wallpaper. It's an unusual and effective way to decorate an upstairs landing, and would look equally effective in any room furnished with antiques.

classic fabrics

Eighteenth-century printed fabrics provide great inspiration to modern textile designers, and any fabric with a traditional floral design will impart a sense of calm and stability to a room. The very first floral fabrics were hand painted using a bamboo brush, or block printed with hand-cut wooden blocks pressed onto the fabric. These were brought to Europe from the Far East in great quantities and proved so popular with the wealthy sections of society for use as furnishing fabrics that there was an embargo on their importation. Finely-drawn one-color prints were made possible only with the invention of copper-plate printing in Great Britain, and the first copper-plate press was probably installed by Christophe-Philippe Oberkampf in France in 1770. The plates were engraved with fine lines cut into the surface which held the color before being pressed tightly against the fabric, thus transferring the color to the cloth. The colors used were predominantly red, purple, and blue.

left: The symbolism of flowers is timeless, and represents the fragility of life itself. Botanically-inspired floral prints remind us of how the bud becomes the flower, and how even the most beautiful things are transient.

right: Blue on a white ground is a classic combination, and used to frame a pretty and unusual arched window, a pair of short curtains gently complements the shape without overwhelming it.

updated antiques

If you are a keen flea-market shopper, you may have come across many an old display cabinet that has seen better days. In a modern white-painted room, a dark mahogany piece of furniture can seem out of place and too heavy, so perhaps you have dismissed them as old-fashioned and not suitable for contemporary living. But take a fresh look at any piece that has pretty moldings or fretwork, and you may find that with a little loving kindness—and a coat of white paint—an old piece of furniture can be given a fresh and contemporary look with a classic twist. French-polished wooden furniture will have a shiny surface that needs to be broken down, so sand carefully before you paint with a good undercoat and a top coat of a water-based acrylic eggshell. Paint the inside of the cabinet with a soft blue for contrast.

left: An assortment of vintage wine glasses and plates are displayed against a background color of soft duck-egg blue inside this refurbished cabinet. The pastel color is seen through the glass, bringing an ethereal quality to the display.

right: This early Victorian cabinet was the perfect size for the narrow landing of an English country house, but the dark wood made it seem overpowering. Now painted white, the delicate tracery of the front panels and decorative molding are seen to best advantage.

grand illusions

Our love affair with the classic, all-white interior has many factors that maintain its continuing popularity. A room painted white—on floor, walls, and ceiling—reflects more light than any other decorating scheme. In southern countries where the light is bright and floods in throughout the year, a brilliant white room can feel dazzlingly cool and serene. In colder northern realms where light is gray and less intense, white often looks better if it is mixed with a hint of color, like brown, gray, or black, to tone it down and remove any hint of blue, but still ensuring that any light is fully maximized.

A room decorated in white has the advantage, too, of allowing furnishings to speak for themselves, without having to compete in terms of color or pattern. Whatever the shade of white, a room painted so simply becomes a bare canvas that can be dressed to reflect many different moods. In this spacious dining room the main elements are all simplicity itself. The tongue-and-groove paneled walls are painted white, bare floorboards are stained with a pale tint, and the furniture is understated and timeless. Natural elements, like sea grass chair seats and a rattan easy chair, make sure that the room reflects the changing tones of nature, with texture as the predominant factor, and its daytime look is simple and elegant. But elements of vivid blue and silver have been brought in for a special dinner party and have changed the essential quality of the space. Nature is still evoked, but it is the sparkling aspect of sun on water that is the inspiration.

above: A large room can be given drama and vivacity with the choice of lighting. This enormous glass chandelier is at variance with the simplicity of the room, but the unexpected touch of glamour adds a theatrical flourish.

left: Here it's the accessories that take the lead, and the scene has been set for a glamorous and stylish table setting by the length of damask-patterned wallpaper used as a center runner. There's no need for elaborate decorations, as the sheen of the silver patterning against the blue is all that is needed.

Laying the table for a special occasion can be creative and satisfying, and using whatever is at hand means you don't need to invest in expensive new tableware. We all make the effort for Christmas and New Year, but a summer birthday party, a silver wedding anniversary, or maybe a supper with friends for no reason at all are all good opportunities to give your dining room a touch of glamour. Stick to a few easy rules, and setting your table for a dinner party will be a good opportunity to use your imagination.

Keep things simple and try not to introduce too many conflicting patterns to the table—there is always enough going on without guests

below: An original artwork will always give a room character and help to underline a color theme. If your budget won't run to the real thing, paint your own on a ready-made canvas using paint tester pots.

having to search for their dessert spoon. A classic white tablecloth is the basic necessity, but a well-ironed linen sheet will serve as an alternative. A decorative runner down the center of the table makes a stunning statement, but it doesn't have to be an extravagant gesture. Try using lengths of wide colored ribbons, a remnant of a favorite furnishing fabric cut into lengths with the ends stitched together, or even a couple of silk scarves placed end to end. Always use classic plain white napkins and plates, and add plenty of basic elements like candles, tea lights, flowers, and sparkling glassware.

below: This summer table was created with classic white china on a plain white background. Co-ordinating the colors turns the setting into something really individual and the theme of blue and silver was dictated by the wallpaper runner.

below right: An uncomplicated table decoration is made from a single flower head laid across each plate—a trick which can be co-ordinated to any scheme by using blooms in the chosen color.

vintage style

above: The simplest ideas are often the most effective, and a pair of blue-and-white Irish linen glass cloths, laid down the center of a table set for lunch, adds color and works as an effective runner.

above right: Vintage style depends on unsophisticated touches, and expensive napkin rings can be replaced by a simple length of jute string tied in a bow with an individual flower head at each place setting.

left: A hand-woven linen sheet makes the perfect white tablecloth for this understated table. Old and new ingredients come together for a relaxed and simple setting that is stylish and elegant.

True classic style means using elements that have stood the test of time, and vintage fabrics and materials are an effortless way to achieve an unpretentious look that can be used every day. Hand-loomed linen tablecloths, embroidered French sheets, and monogramed napkins, all in timeless blue and white, make for an elegant style that is truly ageless. You can often find linen, bone-handled knives, and old silver-plated flatware in antique shops or for sale on internet sites, so build up a collection over time and mix and match with modern glassware and china in traditional shapes.

embroidered history

The art of embroidering threads onto fabric began as early as the Bronze Age in China and Syria; in fact, as long as there has been woven fabric, people have used embroidery as a way to embellish and decorate it. Embroidery has always been an outlet for creativity and has been practised in every culture and country throughout the ages. From the highly embellished and sophisticated silk embroideries of India to the charmingly

below: A wooden sleigh bed, painted white and slightly distressed, has all the simplicity and charm of folk art furniture and the snowy cotton bed linen underlines the look, with its naïve, embroidered design.

below: Four shades of blue—duck egg, aqua, teal, and petrol—are used to bring depth to the machine-embroidered stem-stitch pattern.

below right: A spray of delphiniums in a glass of water beside the bed displays nature's use of color. The petals are finely shaded from the palest tints to deep purple.

naïve samplers worked on linen by young girls in the nineteenth century and the folk art of Eastern Europe, the art of embroidery spans every culture. Modern machine embroidery, using high-tech computers, has made the creation of embroidery incredibly fast compared to the labor-intensive methods of the past, but we are still enchanted by the idea of raised stitches meandering across crisp white cotton.

quilted lines

Stitching two or more layers of cloth together is a time-honored way to make warm, durable fabrics. In Japan, the classic Sashiko stitching technique is a simple running stitch that is sewn in repeating and interlocking patterns and is widely used throughout Asia. In the West, the tradition of quilting arose from the same need to create serviceable home furnishings, and one that reached a peak of creativity with the beautiful "Durham" quilts of the north of England, and the extraordinary quilts of the American folk art tradition.

right: A modern bed quilt has interlocking patterns of machine stitching sewn through two or more layers of fabric. Although relatively inexpensive and found in a chain store, the cover has its roots in a long tradition of classic quilts.

below left: The blue-and-white printed fabric is backed with a co-ordinating stripe, and used for a pair of matching pillow covers.

below: The pastel shades of the quilt fabric, with its leaf and floral motifs, are echoed in the colors of a contemporary printed bedside lampshade.

nostalgic florals

You would be hard pressed to name a single society throughout history that hasn't loved flowers, and in the history of Western culture flowers are gathered in armfuls in paintings, on wall and ceiling decorations, on tapestries, and on woven and printed fabrics. It is an irony that as printing methods developed and floral fabrics became more easily available for everyone, as a society we were becoming more detached from nature. The Industrial Revolution brought technologies that would bring images of the natural world to everyone, but it became a place that for many was only to be visited on high days and holidays.

Of all floral subjects, the rose is the most beloved and in the ancient language of flowers, roses symbolize love and beauty. The most ancient depiction of roses has been found on a fresco at the palace of King Minos, on Crete, dating back more than 3,000 years. These were five-petaled roses, similar to the wild dog rose that we know so well. The Romans and Greeks worshipped the rose,

previous page: A subtle splash of color in this simple bedroom comes from the traditional toile-de-Jouy style fabric dressing the classic white-painted iron bedstead.

left: Delicate garlands of roses are strung around the necks of a collection of 1930s ceramic pitchers that are displayed on a shelf in a classically pretty bedroom.

and used their petals to carpet floors of their rooms during major festivals. Even the Crusaders were known to have brought back many species of roses from the East, and the tradition of transporting roses from far-flung places continued when early tea roses arrived from India in tea clippers.

Throughout the history of design, a few rose motifs have been notable, and in the fifteenth century the rose was used as a symbol for the factions fighting to control England. The white rose symbolized the house of York, the red rose the house of Lancaster, and the struggle between the two was known as the "War of the Roses." Napoleon's wife, Josephine, established an extensive collection of roses at the Château de Malmaison, and her garden became the setting for Pierre-Joseph Redouté's work as a botanical illustrator. His watercolor collection "Les Roses," completed in 1824, is still considered to be the finest collection of botanical illustrations, reproductions of which continue to appear on painted china and as framed prints.

right: Blue roses appear on a set of nostalgically-inspired bed linen. It's a classic design that is always successful when teamed with stripes. Many modern rose growers still strive to produce the perfect blue rose when creating new varieties.

damask blues

When the explorer Marco Polo returned to Venice in 1295 from his travels in Damascus in Syria, he brought with him a shabby bundle of cloths that were woven with a new pattern previously unseen in the West. The revolutionary new fabric was an instant success, and it became known as damask—a woven cloth that is self-patterned and relies on the play of light falling on silken or linen threads to create the design. Damask silks were used as wall coverings in the eighteenth century and papers printed with this elegant and dramatic design are still a great favorite for use as wallpapers and furnishings today.

above: Based on an eighteenth-century French damask-look paper, originally produced in 1793 at St Antoine, this modern reproduction wallpaper has been printed from newly-cut blocks.

right: Used on one wall in a traditional timber-framed house, the sophisticated blue-and-white design makes a fabulous statement against the simple wooden beams and bed frame.

indigo blues

As early as 3,000 BC the plant *Indigofera* was being used in India to produce a deep, permanent blue dye. However, it was not until the sixteenth century that indigo was first introduced to Europe and America where it replaced the original blue dye made from woad. Traditionally, it is work clothes that have been dyed using indigo, and it is to this dye that we owe the characteristic fading of our beloved blue denim jeans. Indigo dyes only the outer coating of a thread, leaving the inner part white, so after repeated washing the inner core is slowly revealed.

below: The depth of indigo blue contrasts vividly with white, and bed linen printed with a dark blue design brings distinction to a brilliant white bedroom. The classic cotton crochet blanket is an all-time favorite and adds to the textural qualities of the room with its American shutters.

Patterned fabrics dyed with indigo use the resist-printing method, a technique opposite to most printing methods where colour is applied to the fabric. In the resist method, fabric is printed with a wax or paste before the fabric is dyed, and it is the wax which stops the dye entering the cloth. The resist material is removed during the last stage of the process, leaving white areas within the blue. Resist-printed techniques have been used in Asia and Africa for centuries, and were introduced to Europe and America during the second half of the eighteenth century. Designs based on them are still popular today.

below: A plain white lampshade is trimmed with round mother-of-pearl sequins that might well have been harvested in the same islands that produced resist-dyed indigo fabrics.

below right: Modern printing methods and dyes mean that this Indonesian-style pattern has been manufactured using synthetic dyes and traditional printing methods, but the design has been influenced by techniques that date back centuries.

vintage blues

In the pale, gray light of northern countries, brilliant whites and vibrant blues can look out of place and cold, as these strong tones need the warm golden light of the south to look their best. For interiors that are not well lit, whose north-facing windows let in a pale, low-key light, seek out blues that are muted, subdued, and quiet. On the far reaches of the blue color palette, gray blues with a hint of green appear relaxed and peaceful.

With its connotations of water, depth, and calm, blue is the obvious color choice for bathrooms, whether it is used for walls and tiles, or for accessorizing a white room. In this classic bathroom in an English farmhouse, the character of the building has been underlined by the choice of traditional bathroom fittings. A reclaimed, roll-top bath from a salvage yard was restored to its former glory when it was re-enameled inside and the exterior painted in a soft, gentle gray-blue. The color is repeated on the walls, and the soft white paintwork on the mirror surround brings a feel of fresh cleanliness.

left: The distressed ball-and-claw feet of the Victorian bath testify to its age. The old cast iron, with its slightly rusting features, is a charming detail in the traditional bathroom.

right: All this bathroom needs is a pair of co-ordinating towels in a matching gray-blue, and a textured bath mat in the same color. The cool tones of the room are warmed by the natural wood of the floor and beams.

left: Stripped floorboards, woodwork, and stairs are all painted in soft heritage blues in the entrance hall of this Gloucestershire country house. The swathe of blue that sweeps along the woodwork and up the curving staircase is offset with walls of off-white.

right: Blue-painted woodwork, and especially window frames, always adds an essentially country look to a room. These traditional French-style windows were bought from a French home store in Calais, ferried home to the English countryside by van, and installed into this converted cow byre.

country blues

The essence of country style is to create rooms that will welcome you home, using delicate color combinations of the natural world—the tranquil blue of a summer sky seen against scudding white clouds, or the serenity of blue forget-me-nots and white wood anemones nodding in a spring garden. These simple images inspire a way of decorating that will bring a taste of country style into your home

accents of blue

Accents of blue in a variety of shades work well in most interiors, but if you are aiming for a relaxed, comfortable room, try to avoid carefully co-ordinated schemes that have no place in a country-style interior. The country look relies for its effect on a mix of vintage accessories that hale from different eras, so scour flea markets and junk stores for tiny flashes of blue-and-white ceramics that can be used along a mantelpiece or shelf. These photos are all details from the room shown on the previous pages.

previous page: With a classic interpretation of the blue and white theme, the walls of this country living room are painted in blue with off-white paintwork. The soft blue comes from an authentic range of paint colors sourced from old country houses. This results in a unique set of colors that looks wonderful in new houses as well as period properties, such as this. But it's the use of fabrics that gives the room its quintessentially country look. Stripes are mixed with naturally-inspired motifs, like cow parsley, fern leaves, and swallows, bringing images and colors of the countryside inside, to be enjoyed in winter as much as on a summer's day. Blues and whites are softened with the natural shades of the Cotswold stone fireplace, and this is reflected in the stone and blue of the fabric on the sofa.

above left: Pick up a door number plate in a flea market and enjoy the deep, rich color of its enameled surface. Originally made in France, these blue and white number plates are seen everywhere on houses in old French towns.

above left : Made in eighteenth-century Holland, Delft tiles can still be bought inexpensively and have a fascinating history. In the seventeenth century, the Dutch East India Company began to import Chinese porcelain, which proved so popular that demand outstripped supply until the factory at Delft began to produce its own range of blue-and-white designs.

above: Combining colors and patterns is easy with a blue and white theme. Soft shades of sky blue, in a selection of designs inspired by nature, give this upholstered bench seat a touch of comfort, and have brought a mix of fabrics by two different designers together with ease.

above right: One of the simplest ways to bring a splash of blue into a country house is by filling a white enamel jug with blue flowers. In winter it's not easy to find a pure blue, but a posy of blue-purple anemones is the right side of blue on the scale and can be found even in the cold months.

Juxtapose a battered antique Delft tile with one-off treasures like a tiny porcelain teapot or an enameled door number plate, and look for pieces of pressed glass that will reflect the colors around them. Build on the range of blues by piling an array of patterned pillows on a sofa or bench to provide a layered effect that will immediately suggest the relaxed comfort of a country house. These are ideas that don't rely on a great deal of money for their execution, but on a keen eye and a love of the unusual.

gingham and stripes

The essence of country living is to create a simplicity of style that allows you to relax and enjoy your home without worrying about formality or over-tidiness.

Country fabrics like ginghams and stripes can be used for unstructured slip covers on sofas and chairs, and are easily mixed and matched without too much regard for co-ordination. In fact, the more layering of tone and pattern, the better. A pillow made from a length of cotton mattress ticking looks unpretentious on a gingham chair, and a checked woolen blanket thrown over the arm of a plain linen sofa piled high with checked and striped pillows looks charmingly unfussy. The beauty of blue and white is that any combination of shades works effortlessly together. Ranging from the greener tones of aqua to the warmer shades of sky blue and ultramarine, placed together in a room they simply suggest the natural world, especially when diluted with copious amounts of white walls and woodwork. Look for country fabrics in natural fibers like cotton and linen, and make long curtains lined with warm interlinings, allowing them to sweep onto the floor for draft-free winter evenings. A chilly country house needs all the help it can get to be cozy and welcoming throughout the year.

left: Long gingham curtains are hung from a narrow black cast-iron pole and frame a long multi-paned window. The antique wooden country chair, upholstered in white linen, epitomizes the understated look.

right: A simple country living room is given a relaxed feel with a blend of different furniture styles and fabrics. Varying tones of blue-and-white patterns are mixed freely together without restraint.

left: Three different fabrics have been used to re-upholster a classic armchair, with a contemporary blue-and-white stripe combined with two different vintage tablecloth fabrics.

above: Flowers captured on fabrics are a constant reminder of nature's infinitely varied pleasures, and the blue-and-white grid pattern on this cotton fabric is decorated with a naturalistic floral design in pinks and greens.

above right: A utilitarian kitchen tablecloth, woven in blue and white, is casually thrown over a small wooden side table. The arrangement is given drama and interest by a contemporary turned wooden sculpture and the flashes of red in the geranium flower and on the 1930s jug.

Blue-and-white fabrics can be charming if mixed with accent touches of pink or red to counteract their coolness. In a country garden room built out from the main house, the walls are whitewashed brick, and vintage fabrics are used to cover hand-me-down furniture, giving the pieces a delightfully nostalgic air. A collection of 1930s and 1940s tablecloths has been used with style and a sense of practicality that sums up the "make do and mend" ethos of the era, as well as the modern necessity for recycling. It's a clever way to bring old pieces to life and to re-use thrift sale finds.

dining with blue and white

Collecting vintage china will always add color and style to your table, especially if you search out a design that was manufactured in a particularly pretty shade. The plates, cups, and saucers on this table were all made at the Poole Pottery in Britain, between 1958 and 1981. Although produced in enormous quantities, the two-color "Twintone" and "Seagull" tableware is not easy to find now, but can still be picked up in charity sales and via internet sites.

right: The two-tone effect of the old china allows pools of soft aquamarine to add color to the white tablecloth. A tiny Victorian cup picks up the color, and adds a tiny spark of accent shades.

below: In this country dining room, the table is all ready to be laid for supper. The dresser in the alcove displays a charming collection of antique pitchers in the same colors as the tableware, giving the room a unified splash of aquamarine against the white of the walls.

modern country

Blue-and-white gingham is an all-time classic, and the freshness and simplicity of this cotton weave has guaranteed the fabric's popularity continuously for over two hundred years. The first cotton ginghams were imported from Indonesia in the seventeenth century, and were originally a simple woven stripe until they started to be produced by the cotton mills of Manchester, England, in the eighteenth century. Woven gingham quickly became a popular fabric, and has been used in interiors as widely diverse as Gustavian Swedish palaces and the simplest country cottages.

Use gingham cotton fabric whenever you want to evoke a country look that is instantly recognizable. Small-scale patterns look pretty and timeless, whereas an over-sized, bold gingham in strong blue and white will instantly appear crisp and contemporary, especially if it's used in an all-white room. In this holiday home in Cape Town, South Africa, the strong morning sunlight is filtered through white-painted American shutters and the contemporary, white-washed dining table and chairs are the epitome of modern country style. Add to the look with stripped wooden floorboards stained with a white sealant, and any room will immediately seem larger than it really is.

left: Nothing could look fresher and more appealing first thing in the morning than a breakfast table laid with a dark blue gingham runner and white china.

top right: A pair of striped dish towels can be cut up and made into a set of napkins, and for a natural napkin ring, look for the rims of shells on seaside walks.

center right: Summer brings a welcome variety of blue flowers. These delphiniums look fresh and simple in a clear glass vase.

right: A seaside tablescape is made up of a branch of driftwood, a tiny wooden boat, and a selection of shells found on the beach. Create a similar effect with treasures collected on a country walk.

simple sophistication

In a small, white-painted American-style clapboard house, the owners have chosen a set of rustic country furniture for the dining room of their weekend bolt-hole. The scrubbed wooden table and teak garden chairs, usually seen outdoors, are combined with a vintage cabinet with a gently weathered appearance. The furniture is simple and the walls

above: The utilitarian cabinet, dating from the 1940s, is plain and unadorned with its wire mesh front panels, but the painted paneling behind adds texture to the corner, and the elegant candelabra makes a stylish statement.

above left: It's a whimsical touch, but bows of blue-and-white striped ribbon tied round each arm of the candelabra link it subtly with the colors of the plates and bowls.

above: Summer sunshine streams in during the late afternoon, and the table is set for an informal meal. In a relaxed holiday house, a tablecloth or place mats seem unnecessary, so the table top is simply scrubbed and laid with the basics.

above right: No fancy napkins or name settings—just a washed pebble and a slip of driftwood in the bowls greet guests for this summer supper, lending the table a spark of originality.

bottom right: A white dish is piled with blueberries and red grapes in the abundance of summer. The raised rim of the dish and shape of the berries provide a rich contrast of color and texture against the washed wood of the tabletop.

painted plain white—a decorating style that works well in houses of this style found around the world. The secret is in the choice of accessories. An ornate cast-iron candelabra adds a touch of glamour on the side cabinet, and the china has been chosen in two shades of blue that add a dimension beyond that supplied by a set of plain white plates and bowls.

naturally
weathered

Exposed to the hot sun and strong salt winds of Cape Town in South Africa, paint is soon blistered and woodwork needs regular maintenance if it's to be kept in pristine condition. Spotted along the coastal road that leads into the city, with its plethora of junk shops and vintage stores, this distressed and well-worn wooden cabinet has obviously see better days, although its precise history is unknown.

If you discover an old piece of furniture, especially if it comes with a low price tag, it can be tempting to imagine it stripped and rubbed down, and perhaps repainted to fit into a contemporary room, but it's far better to take it home and live with it for a while before committing yourself to renovating it. You may find that its layers of peeling paint, the areas that have been partially stripped and left unfinished, and the rusting metalwork communicate a little piece of history that makes it far more interesting to live with.

above: Seen close up, the weatherbeaten paintwork of this old cabinet is as decorative and gritty as any piece of contemporary art or sculpture. The layers of bubbling paintwork reveal the scraped wood beneath, contributing texture and color that a new piece could never achieve.

left: Placed in a contemporary white room, the cabinet is both functional and beautiful. The tattered wooden window shutter has a similar appeal, with its peeling paintwork.

cobalt blues

left: Every country kitchen needs a big wooden table where family meals and informal suppers for friends can be eaten. A crisp white tablecloth and plenty of blue-and-white china are all that is needed to set the scene.

above: A white enamel storage jar with blue lettering has been given a new purpose as it holds a winter-flowering jasmine. In the traditional kitchen, the vintage jar adds just the right note.

above right: Flea markets yield any number of odd side plates for the avid hunter, and a mixed collection of blue and white can be put together to be used everyday.

A red brick inglenook fireplace, exposed wooden beams, and a range stove are hallmarks of the English country kitchen. It's often the heart of the home, where the constant warmth of the stove draws the family together, especially in winter. To balance the heavy tones of wood and brick, this country kitchen has been decorated with plenty of white to make an otherwise potentially dark room fresh and light. The owner's collections of blue-and-white Victorian plates and blue glass medicine bottles add dazzling flashes of cobalt blue that bring to life the traditional interior.

subdued blues

left: With blue walls above and white cabinets below, a gray, granite-effect worktop links the two. The worktop was extended into a small upstand.

below: Tongue-and-groove match-boarding means instant country style. Here it has been painted in the same blue as the plastered walls for continuity.

The combination of blue and white need not necessarily mean a dramatic contrast. Using soft shades of pale gray-blues in conjunction with off-white can result in an airy, relaxed look that echoes wide open spaces and will always make a room appear more spacious. Pale blues bring to mind the expansiveness of a northern summer sky, while white recalls billowing cumulus clouds, so used together the effect is to push away the walls and ceiling,

right: White tulips look fresh and unassuming, while spotted napkins are perfect for use in a country kitchen.

below: The inside of the glass-fronted cabinet has been painted to match the walls, with clear glass shelves to hold wine glasses. Above the plate rack, a collection of hand-thrown pottery pitchers gives a rustic air.

creating an effect of space. You can choose whether to use color on the walls and paint the woodwork white, which is the more conventional approach, or to break from tradition by painting all the walls white and applying color to the woodwork. In this country-style modern kitchen, the owner opted for the hand-made wooden units to be painted in a soft, creamy white, with touches of soft blue on the walls.

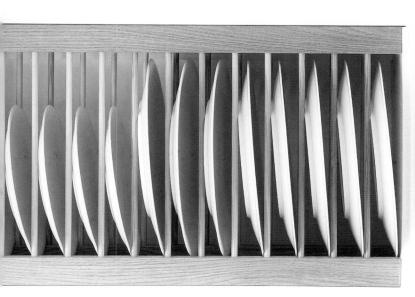

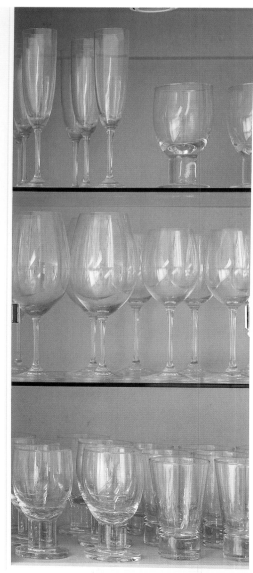

color accents

Even an all-white kitchen can be given blue-and-white style with the addition of a few well-chosen accessories. The tiny white kitchen area in this South African holiday home was built using free-standing units and two wall-mounted cabinets. The decision to paint one of the cabinets a soft gray-blue meant that the corner gained a focal point. Painting all the cabinets to match would have been overwhelming in such a small space, but accents of different blues spark up the mainly white kitchen—the painted wooden cutlery tray, storage jars, and teapot, and even the bright blue nailbrush, found in the supermarket, all help to pull the blue-and-white theme together.

above: With little storage space, the butcher's hooks hanging from the beam mean pots and pans can be stored within arm's reach. A vintage aluminum colander and roasting pans hang side by side with blue enameled kitchenware.

right: Wall cabinets with solid-fronted doors would have felt oppressive above the sink, so the wall units are kept open with wire mesh panels, an integral plate rack, and small display shelves.

country bedroom style

An all-white bedroom in an English country house relies for most of its color on the blue-and-white cottons used on the bed and at the window. The walls and woodwork are unified in their pristine whiteness, and even the accessories on the mantelpiece have a decorative value that is derived more from their texture than anything else. The patterned fabrics are the epitome of country style—long, unlined curtains with an all-over

above: An old country chair and traditional towel rack are the only items that are not blue or white, and the warmth of the natural wood warms up the coolness of the room. Both pieces are of the most modest origins, originally made for a cottage bedroom.

above right: Acquired at a church charity sale, a hand-embroidered cloth is decorated with lazy-daisy and stem-stitch flowers in a range of blues. It is folded and displayed on the wooden towel rack for the simple beauty of its design.

repeating sprig at the window, and a patchwork bedspread lined with Madras check. It's an uncomplicated way to design a bedroom, and one that can be altered as the seasons change without the upheaval of decorating. In under an hour, a pair of summer curtains can be changed for a more substantial set that will keep out winter drafts, and the bedspread layered with a cozy quilt for extra warmth.

childhood blues

Restricted space in a family home often means that children need to share a bedroom, but even in the smallest room it's possible for each child to express their personality. Use color and pattern to mark distinctions by choosing a variety of fabrics for bedcovers, duvets, and pillows. Stripes, spots, floral designs, and novelty prints can be mixed and matched in a blue bedroom so that each child feels they have their own space. In this simple country bedroom, plain wooden beds and bare floorboards were the starting point, making it quick to clean and helping to ease any allergies. Instead of curtains, white wooden shutters filter the light and echo the understated lines of the beds, while the walls were given texture and color with a soft, color-washed effect.

opposite, top left: Customize a plain white lampshade with a blue beaded trim. The beads add a softening effect to the edge of the shade and sparkle in the light.

opposite, top right: The blue color-wash on the walls is simple to achieve with a large brush and one thin coat of paint. Use broad sweeps and keep the brush moving as you apply it.

opposite, bottom left: A sailing print pillow is co-ordinated with stripes for a child who loves boats and the outdoors. The flash of red adds a contrasting touch of color.

opposite, bottom right: Flowers and spots are a classic combination and a rose-printed bed quilt makes a pretty bed for a little girl.

below: Blue walls and white paintwork combine for a fresh and timeless country look. The white-limed beds add a slightly distressed feel that stops them looking too solid.

african country

A classic blue-and-white country look can be adapted and given a warmer, earthier note if it is combined with soft ocher walls, warm wooden furniture, and woven basketwork. In this bedroom in a large country house near Cape Town, the hot earth colors of Africa have been subtly introduced alongside fabrics like blue and white gingham, denim, and a feminine floral print. It's a combination that has resulted in a unique style, reflecting the blue and sand tones of the countryside and shoreline just outside the door, and the ethnicity of materials like

above: The high, beamed ceiling allows air to be circulated by an electric fan and the blue shades of the bed linen inject a coolness that is very welcome at the end of a long, hot summer's day.

above left: Simple country fabrics like denim and striped cottons keep the style understated, while the laced detailing on the denim pillow resonates with the weave of the basketwork shade.

above: A capacious storage unit holds towels and summer clothing in roomy natural baskets. The choice of gingham window dressings keeps the style unadorned and simple, and plays a major role in giving the bedroom its easy country style.

the woven lampshade and storage baskets. The essence of true country style is this reflection of nature and the environment.

In cool, northern-hemisphere countries, where outdoor shades are pale and muted, blues work best if they are gray-toned, or contain just a hint of lavender. Whites are tinged with an undertone of gray, too. However, in the southern hemisphere, with its hot terra cotta, burnt clay, and brilliant blues, whites are bright and tinged with blue to reflect heat from the dazzling sunlight.

embroidered cottons

The shapes and colors of nature have always inspired designers of country fabrics, and the tradition of Indian hand-embroidered fabrics is no exception. In time-honored Indian embroidery, threads were dyed in natural colors, and the use of too many colors in the same fabric was usually avoided. These days, mass-production trends mean that most embroidered fabrics are manufactured by sophisticated computer-driven machines, but the flamboyant and beautiful designs are often inspired by ancient floral motifs and have a resonance with the Indian culture of highly decorative design.

above left: Emulating a fabric decorated with hand stitching, a modern sheer is seen at its best held against the light for the full beauty of the design to be appreciated.

above: Found in a homeware store far away from the source of the fabric, this lampshade has a stylized flower motif that almost exactly matches those on the bed drapes.

right: Draped over a mosquito net hung from the ceiling, the sheer embroidered fabric makes a beautifully simple set of bed drapes that brings glamour to an otherwise minimal scheme. The blues in the stitching are echoed by the plain tones of the curtains and pillow.

contemporary country

In the development of modern bathroom design, a classic-contemporary style has emerged that is used by interior designers and architects alike. Large, natural travertine or limestone tiles used on walls and flooring are combined with sleek white sanitary ware with cutting edge design. It's a timeless look that has become a blueprint for many wet rooms, showers, and bathrooms worldwide—in relaxed country houses as well as chic city apartments. There's nothing quite like the natural ambience of natural stone, and bathrooms have become a sanctuary in the home where comfort and contemplation combine with practicality. While cool and refreshing in hot countries, in colder climes you can combine stone floors with warming under-floor heating.

right: A contemporary en-suite shower room in this South African home has been given color and texture with woven storage baskets and folded blue and white towels. The main bedroom with its blue window curtains is reflected in the mirror, linking the two rooms with their complementary shades of blue.

below left: Dark wood furniture underlines the essentially modern nature of the shower room, but the stained bamboo towel rack is hung with country-style striped towels, and adds a rustic flavor.

below: A white ceramic basin is set on top of a concrete unit, and stainless steel faucets are fixed directly into the wall and mirror above. It's a definitive twenty-first-century bathroom design, but the open shelves allow African baskets to add an ethnic touch.

touches of blue

The beauty of this all-white shower room lies in its essentially practical nature. Easy to clean and a dream to maintain, it's a simple, elegant solution to bathroom design. The painted wooden units and contemporary square basin might be expected to belong to a small city apartment, but in fact the shower room is part of the guest suite in an English country house. Using hand-blocked linens in blue and white, the owner has augmented the clean lines with softly draped fabrics that have alleviated the sharp lines of the room. A length of striped linen has been simply pegged over a standard white shower curtain and left to drape on the floor, while the waterproof curtain behind keeps water in the shower tray. It can be difficult to find stylish shower curtains but using a patterned fabric top curtain neatly solves the problem.

left: A white-painted vintage mirror and trimmed hand towel combine with the fabric shower curtain to bring a country flavor to the minimal design of the shower room.

right: A hand-blocked, floral motif in blue used as a decorative trim gives a standard white hand towel a personalized touch.

left: Using an age-old technique of lime plaster colored with mineral pigments, the wall leading to a bathroom in a Moroccan interior glows with the intensity of sapphire blue.

right: Although simply executed, the opening between the two rooms is formed by an inset archway, the quintessential shape of Moroccan architecture which is found on doorways, windows, and minarets.

jewel blues

Within the glamour of a jewel box, the dazzling colors of precious and semi-precious gem stones can be found in every shade of blue, the most mysterious seen in the richness of blue sapphires and lapis lazuli, the most brilliant in the stunningly beautiful turquoise. From cerulean to cobalt, Prussian blue to azure, the earliest blue pigments used for paints were extracted from minerals found deep in the earth.

plaster finishes

In the ancient walled city of Marrakech in Morocco, many of the older houses, called riads, were built around a central courtyard. Hundreds of these have been recently updated, given swimming pools and smart roof terraces, and turned into fashionable and stylish hip hotels. The use of tadelakt, the polished wall finish traditionally used in bath houses, has undergone a huge revival, along with many other traditional crafts. Wall surfaces are troweled in a plaster made of powdered limestone mixed with colored pigments. The plaster is then polished hard with flat river stones, sealed with a glaze of egg white, and polished again with black olive soap. This results in a beautifully waterproof surface that can be used in showers and bathrooms, but is so beautiful with its texturally smooth and crackled surface that it is now used extensively in contemporary Moroccan interiors.

left: This white shower enclosure and the blue of the interior walls are all finished in tadelakt, illustrating that the technique is as versatile as the pigments that color it.

right: A traditionally-shaped archway has been built into the wall above the bed in this typically Moroccan bedroom. Bed linen, throw, walls, and curtains are all intense shades of plain blue, resulting in a richly colorful experience.

traditional tiling

The interiors of old Moroccan houses were designed to keep out the heat and to provide total privacy from the bustling and noisy streets outside. Walking through the dark and narrow labyrinthine alleys of Marrakech, some so low it is necessary to bend as you walk, it is impossible to imagine how lavish and beautifully ornamented are many of the interiors hidden behind heavy, studded wooden doors. Within, rooms inside the outer walls are dark and cool with no external windows and are generally lit from above. In contrast, any room that faces out onto the central courtyard garden is filled with light and sunshine.

This modern bathroom in a traditional riad in the medina, or old town, is lit only by a high skylight, and no attempt has been made to make the room look bright and light. This subtle lighting only serves to intensify the deep tones of the hand-made tiles. Originally the room may have been part of a suite inhabited by one family unit, but today it is a modern ensuite bathroom with all modern conveniences deftly concealed within the traditional decorations.

left: The bath itself is constructed of bricks, and plastered outside with waterproof tadelakt plaster, while the inside, as well as the surround and the floor, is completely covered with hand-made tiles in rich shades of blue.

above: The streets of the Marrakech souks, or markets, are lined with fascinating stalls selling everything from leather slippers to highly desirable jewelry and metal lanterns, like this one with blue stained-glass panels. In some areas it is possible to watch artisan craftsmen at work as they make modern designs using ancient traditions.

right: Made in the traditional way, using techniques unchanged for hundreds of years, each tile in this bathroom is slightly different in shade from its neighbor, resulting in a mosaic-like effect.

new from old

French architect Charles Boccara has been instrumental in reawakening many traditional Moroccan building techniques in the latest upsurge of development in Marrakech. Using age-old elements like arches, carved woodwork, and intricate mosaic work, but giving them a fresh, modern twist, Boccara set an example with his world-famous Les Deux Tours, the stylish boutique hotel set in the Palmerai area outside the city. The time-

above left: In a spacious courtyard, blue tiles are set out in intricate patterns that resemble designs found in ancient palaces like the Alhambra in Spain, built during the Islamic flowering of arts and architecture.

above: In a typically traditional-looking bathroom, inspired by public bath houses, this polished plaster bath is surrounded by walls of blue and white tiles with a distinctively Moroccan use of color.

above: As intricate zellije tiling is extremely expensive to produce, a small area is decorated in front of a plaster fireplace to resemble a rug on the floor, and the arch of the fireplace is similarly ornamented. The soft blue tiles inject subtle accents of color into a room dressed in white linen.

honored craft of making zellije, or mosaic tiles, is continued to this day in the city of Fez. Tiles are made from sunbaked clay, dipped in rich enamel colors, and fired before being cut into intricate shapes, the designs of which have been handed down from father to son for generations. Zellije has been taken to a fine art at Les Deux Tours, with flooring, walls, and even fireplaces decorated with this ancient technique.

artisan crafts

In the seventeenth and eighteenth centuries, Moroccan artisans made their living by producing beautiful furniture, woodwork, and ceramics for royal palaces and mosques. Today, craftsmen address themselves to the demands of the wealthy, and more recently to the influx of tourists. The major cities have specialist quarters for the production of different crafts, with well-regulated guilds that preserve the highest standards of workmanship through a rigorous apprenticeship system. Different cities will produce similar-looking products, like the ceramics made in Fez and Safi, while sustaining enough difference in the choice of colors to keep their individuality. The recent demands of the tourist industry have

above: Specially commissioned for the Villa Maroc in the seaside town of Essaouira, this blue-and-white dinner service is hand-painted in a pattern based on traditional motifs. Young apprentices are employed for hand painting simple designs, gradually moving on to more complex and intricate pieces as they acquire higher skills.

above left: A mosaic table is typical of Moroccan garden furniture, with its metal base. Hand-cut blue and white zellije shapes are made from larger tiles made in Fez, the major producer of this type of ceramic tile.

above: The Atlantic coastal region is known as Al Jorfal Asfar, or "the Yellow Coast," because of the yellowish clay found there. This is used for the production of the distinctive blue-and-white ceramics made at Safi, where large quantities of bowls and plates are made.

above right: Pillows are covered in a fabric printed in Provence in France, using antique blocks inspired by Indian cottons. This is not a traditional Moroccan design, but the simple blue patterning is perfectly in tune with the local woven fabrics and the designs found on ceramics. Silk fabrics, woven in Marrakech, are made into tasseled scarves for beautiful fashion accessories.

involved changes, and new forms and styles have emerged that are based on traditional designs.

Blue and white has been used in the decoration of Moroccan ceramics since the thirteenth century, and in the mid-nineteenth century a dramatic cobalt blue was introduced, which is still popular today. The city of Fez is most famous for its blue-and-white pottery, known as Bleu de Fez, or Moroccan Blue. Originally the color became predominant because of the large deposits of cobalt to be found in the rocks and stones swept down by the rivers, which were ground to provide the blue powder used in glazes.

the hand of fatima

On many of the massive studded entrance doors that abound in medieval Moroccan cities you can find intricate metal door knockers, shaped as the age-old protective symbol of a hand. This symbol, often called the hand of Fatima, is said to ward off the evil eye, which in Morocco today is still seen as an important force.

Fatima was the compassionate daughter of the Prophet Mohammed, and miracles have been attributed to her; one being that when she prayed in the desert it began to rain. The hand is also called a "khamsa," meaning five in Arabic, which refers to the five fingers on the hand. The hand of Fatima is used throughout the Middle East and parts of Africa as a symbol of protection, and is also often worn as an amulet on a pendant around the neck. In this contemporary conversion of an old house in Marrakech, the symbol of the hand has been reproduced in plaster as wall decorations, and hung on a sapphire blue wall. It's a striking and decorative way to bring the ancient symbols of the Moroccan and Islamic culture into a contemporary setting.

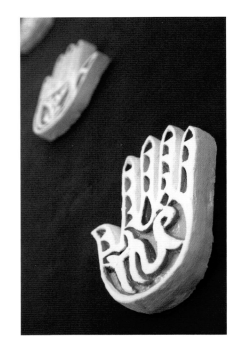

above: The strong contrast of bold color and pure brilliant white immediately draws the eye, bringing a sense of drama to the room.

right: Set against a white wall, a pair of sofas are upholstered in jewel-blue stripes and separated by a traditional Moroccan-style table. Strong, sweet mint tea, poured from a metal teapot and served in small glasses, is always offered to guests.

berber weaves

Textile weaving in Morocco is the greatest of the artistic traditions, and also one of the most ancient. Traditional techniques have been preserved for centuries and handed down through the generations, mainly because weaving and embroidery have always been an essential part of daily life, and also because they are believed to act as a source of magic and power. The simple geometric designs include many traditional symbols designed to ward off evil spirits and bring good luck.

above: The most widely-used motifs are the hand of Fatima and the eye, which are represented in woven textiles by a variety of crosses, triangles, and lozenges. These woven textiles are looked upon as a talisman, affording protection against evil.

right: Rugs and blankets are often woven in vibrant, jewel-like colors, designed to offset the dimly lit houses in villages and cities. Here a woolen rug, woven in colors to link the bed linen and walls, is used as a window shade in a contemporary bedroom.

color it blue

Painting one wall in a vivid color is a spectacular way to add character and individuality to an otherwise bland room. Many newly-built houses and apartments are sadly lacking in architectural features, and where a beautiful window frame, an interesting ceiling shape, or a paneled wall in an older property asks only for an overall coat of a single color, a square, boxy room can be immediately enhanced with color applied to one of the walls. It's a quick way to bring blue and white together in a scheme, and although it's possible to successfully accessorize a completely white room with blue pillows, throws, and rugs, a feature wall of blue will always look dramatic.

You can use color to apparently change the dimensions of a room, too. A small room can be made to look much bigger with walls painted in a pale, airy sky blue, while dark blue applied to the ceiling of a high room will make it appear lower. Use deep cobalt blue on the end walls of a long, thin room and it will seem to have more balanced proportions. When you are choosing paint shades, always buy tester pots first, and try out the color on a large sheet of paper. Before you finally decide, hold the sheet up on different walls, and observe how the light, both natural and artificial, changes the color.

right: A white wrought-iron day bed stands out against a wall of rich, inky blue where its lines are contrasted against the rich color. An indigo and white patchwork quilt helps to unite the diversity of tones.

left: Match a collection of vintage brooches to the fabric of the pillow. Here, a silk pillow in pale blue has been trimmed with beads and makes a shimmering backcloth to the sparkling glass of the jewelry.

right: A utility fabric like this blue cotton denim makes a serviceable pillow on which a display of quite ordinary buttons has been sewn. It's the random patterning and the contrast of matt and shiny textures that add a charming appeal.

bejeweled furnishings

Customizing a pillow is a creative way of adding individuality and imaginative flair to a room, and is a small enough project for experimentation without much expense. Stitch a collection of ribbons, buttons, badges, and beads to a ready-made pillow cover, or make your own in a fabric that co-ordinates with the rest of the room. Look for decorative details in sewing stores, where you can find a large and tempting selection of beaded trims and buttons, or scour junk shops and charity sales for interesting pieces of old costume jewelry.

left: On the Cape Peninsula in South Africa, ocean waves have had the whole breadth of the Atlantic Ocean to gather intensity before the surf rolls in and crashes on the beach. It's a dramatic place to sit with a glass of wine and catch the salt spray.

right: A white-painted Adirondack-style bench seat sits on a wooden balcony high above an ocean view, its hard seat softened by a pair of co-ordinating blue-and-white striped pillows that perfectly embody coastal style.

coastal blues

The ever-changing nature of the ocean can bring tranquillity with calm, sparkling days or engage all the senses with its wild excesses of crashing waves—and blue and white predominate. From the aquamarine, turquoise, and cerulean of a rolling Atlantic breaker with its white foaming surf, to the luminous azure and ultramarine of the glittering deep, the colors of the sea will always inspire.

95

al fresco eating

On summer evenings by the ocean, eating outside is one of life's great pleasures. Relaxing within sight and sound of the roaring surf, city stresses drop away, and energy can be replenished with good food and a glass of wine with friends. Outdoor tables need only the most informal settings for al fresco suppers, and hardwood furniture, with the silvery patina acquired from exposure to sizzling summer sun and onshore winds, needs only a simple woven runner and understated white china to prepare it for the evening to come.

One of the most popular woods used for garden furniture is teak. This dense tropical hardwood is full of natural oils that make it highly resistant

above: A set of silvery teak furniture is laid with blue and white to reflect the colors of the sea that acts as a backdrop to this beach-side deck. Strong winds can blow off the ocean, and the checked runner is held in place by a pair of heavy stones placed on either end.

previous page: In this beach house on the coast just outside Cape Town, the ocean is a mere stone's throw away so the colors of sea and sky inform the choice of interior furnishings. Glass doors to the living room fold back and the boundaries between the dramatic shoreline and the house disappear.

above: When the drama of ocean breakers is so close, sophistication is unnecessary. Even if you live miles from the sea, use whatever you have at hand to decorate a seaside-style table; here, stones and fragments of driftwood picked up from the beach and low candles are piled in a local, hand-carved wooden bowl.

above right: Fragile nautilus shells, found in abundance on winter beaches in the Cape Peninsula, add a charming finishing touch to a pure white table setting.

to all weather conditions, and although very expensive, it will last for a lifetime or more. The rise in the popularity of teak has led to ecologically sound production in the last few years, but it's always worth checking where it has been sourced. Left outside in the sun, it takes about six months for teak to change from brown to a silvery gray, but if you prefer to keep its natural color, scrub with hot soapy water and a non-metalic brush, and oil it every year with a rub-down of teak oil. Teak that has been left to turn gray still needs care, so brush it down every spring with a solution of dishwashing liquid and a little bleach in a bucket of hot water and oil it every five years or so.

Ideal for a sunny spot on a windy deck, wrought-iron garden furniture is heavy enough to stay in place during stormy weather. Find vintage pieces at garage sales or salvage yards, and renovate them with a wire brush and can of car spray paint. Typically decorated with curlicues and arabesques, wrought iron needs regular cleaning and maintenance if it isn't to rust, especially when exposed to salt spray. Similar in style but much more lightweight, aluminum furniture is more suitable for a sheltered spot out of the wind, but is durable throughout the year.

left: A cast-iron table has been enhanced with blue-and-white mosaic for a decorative finish. Make your own with flat pieces of broken china fixed with tile adhesive and then grouted. A set of painted tiles or even a vintage plate will yield patterned china for using as mosaic.

right: Perfect for a leisurely breakfast while keeping a lookout for whales and dolphins out at sea, two elegant cast-iron chairs have a pair of faded seat pads tied on for extra comfort. Sturdy linen or canvas fabric is ideal for use here, as it can withstand any amount of strong sunlight.

nautical flavor

Coastal living isn't only about shimmering days on sunny decks and gazing out across the azure ocean. Even in sunny climates, winter days can be chilly and a winter fireplace is needed for when a bit of cozying up is required. But the sea isn't out of mind even when the family close the doors and sit round a log fire. The solid wooden mantelpiece is garnished liberally with nautical

above: Robust wooden furniture in natural tones echoes the nautical flavor of the house, and brings warmth and texture to a winter living room. A pair of armchairs is upholstered in durable white linen covers that can be removed and laundered regularly, making them a practical choice for family living.

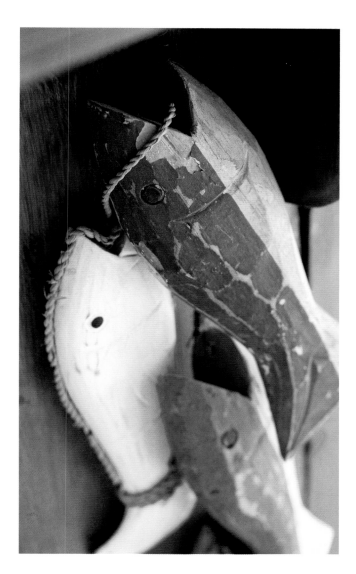

above: Locally carved wooden fish are painted in tones of blue and white, and then distressed to look like sea-washed flotsam. Most coastal towns have a history of fishing, and homeware shops abound with similar fish-inspired accessories.

above right: Striped fabrics come in many guises, from plain mattress ticking to more complex combinations of stripes and plains. When the underlying color scheme is blue and white, layering them together is an unbeatable combination for the coastal look.

objects—a large wooden model of a sailing ship, carved wooden fish hanging from a line, and shells and starfish picked up on winter beaches when the storms toss up a hoard of treasures. Combined with fabrics chosen in sea-faring stripes of blue and white, it's a sure-fire way of giving even a land-locked living room a taste of the ocean.

cape cod style

With stunning views of the incredibly diverse South African fine bush (or "fynbos" in Afrikaans), with the Atlantic Ocean behind, the interior of this tiny wooden weekend house has deliberately been kept as minimal and as simple as possible so that the outdoor landscape takes center stage. The fynbos is the natural shrub land of the south-east coast of Africa, and forms part of the beautiful Cape floral kingdom. It's a wonderful natural planting that creeps right up to the house and outdoor decking.

Set in a nature reserve, this wooden house is white-painted in a style reminiscent of America's Cape Cod style and is shingled with a corrugated iron roof. The two easy chairs that furnish the living area of the open-plan ground floor are upholstered in a muted gray-blue fabric—soft shades deliberately chosen to blend with the colors of nature. They face out to sea at all times, encouraging family and friends to relax and fully observe the glorious outlook. A silent watcher can sometimes see small bush buck and lizards near the deck, but from June to December, Southern Right whales and Humpbacks come very close inshore to breed and mate. These placid, gentle giants can be easily seen from the house as they approach the beach just a short walk away.

left: The polished concrete floor gleams throughout the lower floor of the house. It's easy to keep clean when sandy feet trail through, and is softened by the natural woolen rugs under the chairs.

In such a small house, open-plan living keeps the rooms airy and cool in the height of the sweltering South African summer. With sliding doors wide open to the sea, and the front door propped open, a fresh breeze straight from the sea is encouraged to blow through the living room and tiny kitchen. The wooden structure is open to the roof, with stairs that rise up from the living area to the bedroom in the apex of the roof. Exposed ceiling joists, stairs, and walls are all painted brilliant white, a feature which adds to the sense of space and coolness and unifies the bare bones of the structure. The only color is provided by the blue stripes and gingham of the upholstery and pillows, and the flashes of blue in the kitchen.

The simple style is very much inspired by the beach houses of Cape Cod in the USA, with their tradition of blue-and-white stripes and sea-faring history. The house is newly-built, but narrow painted tongue-and-groove boards have been fitted all the way around the lower half of each room—a sure way to say vintage seaside style, and one that can be emulated to give character and texture to boxy, new-build rooms.

above: A unified theme of blue and white means you can mix large and small checks together with a variety of stripes when you layer up pillows on a chair or sofa.

left: A free-standing unit with a built-in hob separates the kitchen from the main living area. It's a neat solution to keeping the kitchen apart, without sacrificing the necessary space, and allows the cook to be in touch with the view at the same time.

wide-open spaces

This house is designed to take full advantage of the surrounding landscape, and many of the rooms open out onto their own area of private deck. Folding doors make it all possible, and guests who are early risers love the arrival of the dawn light, but not everyone appreciates being woken at daybreak in summer. For them, the owners

previous page: A wooden house faces the ocean with doors that have been designed to fold back on two sides of the building. Occupants can see verdant hills, sweeping sand dunes, and crashing surf, all from the bedroom. A shallow pool laps the concrete terrace, and bathers can descend into the deeper plunge pool for a refreshing dip.

above: Although the spaces and fittings are lavish in their apparent simplicity, the four-poster bed has been made from the most modest of materials. Reclaimed wooden posts, still with vestiges of paint attached, have been formed into a base with an unadorned frame that makes the most of the high-ceilinged room.

above right: There is no need for fabric hangings around the bed, as the main requirement is to allow cool drafts to waft across sleepers on hot, airless nights. A garland of white starfish threaded onto scrim makes an understated decoration.

have installed blackout curtains that hang behind the fine white cotton drapes which reach to the floor and effectively keep the light at bay until it is wanted. Color is minimal, although a plain cotton duvet cover in soft aqua and a pair of toning pillow covers are all that's needed to bring the shades of the sea into the room.

coastal bathing

It is surely one of life's luxuries to have space enough in a bedroom for a free-standing bath in the corner from which you can leisurely survey the surrounding landscape. But even if the view is more limited, immersing yourself in scented bubbles in the bedroom makes bath time into something really special. A contemporary, natural stone bath looks as smooth as a pebble, reminiscent of sea-washed rocks on the coastline, with its rounded edges and pod-like structure, and does away with any hint of the utilitarian.

The modern love affair with natural stone began with the ubiquitous use of floor and wall tiles, and has now become almost obligatory for bathroom design in both traditional and contemporary interiors. Stone in the bathroom is one of the most ancient of bathroom fittings—the Romans loved to bathe communally in bath houses paved with marble and thought a daily bath was essential to health—and is now one of the most up-to-date materials you can choose. Stone baths can be sourced in hand-carved limestone or even marble, making them an expensive but fabulous option. Stone composite is a newer material, made of a mix of stone particles, marble, and resin. Baths made of composite are lighter in weight than real stone, hold the heat well, and are versatile and durable.

left: This oval stone composite bath is raised on a dais for bathers to take full advantage of the wonderful view of the surrounding coastline.

below: Bringing the outside in—a cast-iron peg rail holds bathrobes for all the family, announcing the fact that the beach is just outside the door.

bathroom blues

In a newly-built seaside house, a white bathroom is given interest and texture with a bath panel and splashback made from pale, watery blue glass mosaic tiles. The tiles are both functional and decorative, protecting the walls and bath panel from water damage, and bringing a beautifully iridescent surface to relieve the white walls.

The history of mosaic goes back over 4,000 years, but it was not until the rise of Byzantium (modern Istanbul, in Turkey), in 500 AD, that glass mosaic was first used. Intricate walls and ceilings were decorated with small glass tesserae called smalti, and these were often backed with silver or gold, set at a slight angle and left ungrouted, so that they glittered and sparkled as the viewer moved around. The use of mosaic panels in bathrooms today is a fashionable and contemporary tiling choice, and blue is always popular, with its suggestions of sea and sky, but all-over mosaic can be expensive. Get a flavor of the look with a narrow border of blue mosaic set above a splashback of plain ceramic tiles, or inset a strip of mosaic within a tiled wall. Most glass and ceramic mosaic tiles are available glued onto a paper or mesh backing, making it easy to fix them to the wall and doing away with the tedious chore of precisely setting out hundreds of tiny tiles.

above: A white and blue bathroom in a coastal holiday home is co-ordinated with a selection of plain and spotted towels and a striped rag-rug bath mat, all in a variety of different blues.

left: The angular lines of the deep bath tub and the square shelves are echoed by the tiny glass tesserae that line the walls. A softer note is added by the collection of sea urchin shells picked up at the beach.

left: A traditional Moroccan studded door has been given a fresh coat of bright blue paint and adds character to a newly constructed wall of pink mud bricks in a courtyard garden of the Palmerie, outside Marrakech.

right: Behind the white-painted tracery of a wrought-iron grille, a blue-painted window folds back against a carved wooden shutter, giving three layers of protection from the world outside while still bringing a gleam of the blue sky into the room.

outdoor blues

Reflecting the tones of the sea and sky, blue is one of nature's favourite colors and always gives a sense of wide-open spaces. Use blue outside for splashes of color that reflect the shades of your favorite blue flowers, from the vividness of periwinkles and delphiniums to the deep purple tones of violas and pansies.

garden retreat

Making a space outside to sit and appreciate the delights of eating in the open air is one of life's pleasures, but blue skies are not always guaranteed and if the heavens darken and rain threatens it can be safer to set up under shelter. In changeable weather, make the most of a covered area where you can lay the table with white linen and blue-and-white china and enjoy an informal meal. This can be as effortless as a cup of tea and a slice of cake in the afternoon, or a relaxed evening supper with candles and lanterns to light up the dusk. Setting up in a covered arbor, an old barn, or even a tidied-up glasshouse will make sure you are out of the wind and stay dry. Keep the ambience casual by searching for old garden furniture, such as a set of slatted park chairs or a bare wooden tabletop on metal trestles.

left: In an old barn used as a potting shed and garden store, the wooden walls have turned silvery-gray with age. The pristine whiteness of the vintage linen and the prettiness of the blue-and-white china make a startling contrast and transform this into an inviting place for a relaxed tea time.

right: Mixed shades of blue hydrangea heads appear soft and mellow against the pale wooden wall behind, yet they add a touch of formality to the corner with its terra cotta pots of succulents.

blue paintwork

Renovating an old property requires thought and sensitivity to the history of the building. Here a set of derelict barns set deep in the Gloucestershire countryside had been used as a cow byre for years before they were converted into a long, low, rambling family home. The Cotswold stone that it is built from is warm and mellow, and the original one-storey construction has been left to look very much as it had been for a century when viewed from the outside. Bedrooms and bathrooms are tucked under the eaves, with roof lights set into the old tiles. On the ground floor, double doors have been let into the deep stone walls all around, leading out onto the garden and the inner courtyard and allowing access to the outside from all areas of the house. The owners chose blue for all the external paintwork for its echoes of summer skies, and the overall effect is of a beautiful old French farmhouse.

left: In an English country garden, planting can be relaxed and blowsy, like these purpley-blue and white violas. The flowers are growing in weathered terra cotta pots and fall over the edges of a white wirework container.

right: External paintwork needs to withstand the rigors of the weather, so it is important to choose the right paint. Exterior paint needs to be flexible and durable, resistant to peeling and flaking and yet still allow the wood to breathe. These French doors are painted with an eggshell finish in a blue heritage paint color that is in total accord with the style of the house.

above: Worn by centuries of hands, the wood is rubbed bare and the ancient metalwork is rusty and broken. These signs of wear testify to the house's heritage and only serve to enhance the romance.

above right: Most of these tiles have been in place for many years, and the oldest have been faded by the sun to a pale imitation of their former glory. Where necessary, replicas have been made and the walls restored with empathy and a light touch.

left: Around the door, the years have done their work, fading the wooden door to the palest gray and leaving behind a mere wash of the cobalt blue paint that would have once looked so fresh and new.

In a five-hundred-year-old Moroccan riad, or garden house, a weathered door to the original well has lost all but traces of its original paintwork. The house is in one of the poorest areas of the Marrakech medina, and was almost falling down when it was bought as a vacation home by a European family. Rather than restore it to a gleaming pastiche, the present owner's decision to preserve as much as he can gives the house a unique mood that is full of character and local color.

urban retreat

At Riad Edward, a chic boutique hotel in Northern Marrakech, pink-plastered roof terraces that would once have been home to goats, chickens, and lines for drying laundry have been restored and are used by guests seeking a calm retreat from the chaotic clamor of the old town just outside the door. The roof is a secluded world of its own, with cushioned resting places under cover, a sunbathing deck with white canvas awnings, and fascinating views across rooftops. Small, intimate corners make sheltered places to breakfast before the sun gets high, but five times a day the air rings with the sonorous tone of the muezzin calling the faithful to prayer. The sound of donkeys braying, families quarreling, and children laughing drift up from the city below, along with the scent of wood smoke, and add to the richly sensuous mix of color, sound, and smell that is Marrakech.

left: Traditional artisan crafts are readily available everywhere in the city and the wrought-iron grilles, made almost on the doorstep, adorn every window and make it possible to leave windows open through the hot summer nights.

right: As in so many houses in Morocco, blue is used for much of the outdoor paintwork and furniture. The heavy studded door, the window surround, and the tabletop made from lime-plaster tadelekt all resonate with the rich blue of the Moroccan sky.

villa maroc

Driving from Marrakech to the coastal town of Essaouira, there is a point along the road where the color of the buildings changes abruptly from warm pink brick to blue and white, where the earthy colors of the desert are replaced by the colors of the sea and sky. Villa Maroc is one of the most fascinating small riad hotels in Essaouira, situated just inside the town ramparts, whose blue-painted balconies, whitewashed terraces, and spectacular views of the ocean are in contrast to the dark, intimate salons where guests eat traditional Moroccan food on low divans by lamp and candle light.

far left: In Mediterranean countries, painting doors and windows blue is a traditional way to keep away evil spirits, who are supposedly attracted by the color and are thus prevented from entering the house.

left: A bedroom window opens on to the wide main street of the town, whose buildings are dazzling in their whiteness. The ubiquitous blue window shutters help keep summer heat out of rooms by day and the long windows allow in plenty of air by night.

right: Villa Maroc has been converted from five merchant's houses, each one with its own open courtyard garden. Rooms are arranged around these courtyards on three levels in the traditional Moroccan manner, where dining rooms and bedrooms are kept cool in summer and warmed in winter with open wood fires.

majorelle blue

All over Marrakech you can find a deep, vibrant blue made famous by the French artist Jacques Majorelle. In 1919 Majorelle visited Morocco and immediately fell in love with this city, later buying land outside the old medina where he based his studio, surrounding it with a delightful garden. The garden was open to the public, but after his death in 1962, it fell into disrepair until discovered by Yves Saint Laurent. YSL bought it with his partner, Pierre Bergé, and restored it to its former glory. The gardens have now been reopened for all to visit and enjoy, and Majorelle's studio, now a tiny museum, has a fine collection of Islamic arts and crafts on display.

The deepest cobalt, Majorelle blue has become synonymous with the artist, and the gardens are rich with walls, balconies, and urns all painted in this heart-stopping color. Look in any hardware store in the city and you'll find tins of the Majorelle blue paint that were used on the walls of this private courtyard with its own plunge pool. It's a blue so intense that the saturated color of the Moroccan sky looks pale in comparison.

left: Opening onto the private courtyard, a wooden door has panels of blue stained glass. The door is kept ajar by a locally-made urn that has been painted in the same Majorelle blue as the walls.

right: A wrought-iron day bed is padded with white canvas pillows that have a startling effect against the vivid blue of the walls. Ideal for reclining after a plunge in the blue mosaic pool, the day bed is made in the simple vernacular style so beloved of local artisans.

blue waters

Swimming is not a traditional Moroccan activity, the local preference being for a visit to the single-sex Hammam, or bath house. A weekly visit to these hot steam rooms, a gossip with friends, and a massage is still enjoyed by locals. But with the influx of tourists comes the need to provide them with a few luxuries of modern life. The boutique hotels that have sprung up in Marrakech and other Moroccan cities are noticeably lacking in mini bars, air conditioning, or telephones in the bedrooms, preferring instead to make guests feel as if they are staying in a private house. But in the scorching heat of the summer, a cool dip is felt to be obligatory by Westerners. The riads that have been converted into guest houses would originally have had at their center a cool garden or courtyard, with a splashing water fountain and tiled floors, but many new owners have taken the decision to remove the fountain, not without much heart-searching, and replace it with a swimming pool.

left: A contemporary white-tiled plunge pool is cool and inviting in the hot sun. The rounded, Roman end with its shallow steps makes it a safe place for children to splash, and for adults to sit and wallow in the reviving blue water.

right: At Riad Edward, the decision to remove the original fountain was not taken lightly, but the charm of the courtyard is assured by the presence of the ancient Cyprus tree whose leafy branches are visited by countless birds and which shades the swimming pool. The ubiquitous sweet mint tea, offered at all times of day and night, is served from a silvery pot and is made with fresh mint bought in the local street market.

above: The tiling of this fountain has a thousand years of history behind it with its small tiles of rich blue. It is a perfect example of the type of fountain that would have graced the interior of the traditional courtyards in the city.

left: The white marble column, topped by a hand-carved bowl, supports a metal fountain of constantly trickling water that adds an ageless quality to the formal layout of the garden.

It's not unusual to find several houses in the old quarter of Marrakech knocked together to make one larger residence. At Riad Enija, three houses once belonging to a silk merchant from Fez—and 64 members of his family!—have been converted into a veritable palace with a fabulously intricate warren of rooms, courtyards, stairways, and roof terraces. The largest courtyard houses an exotic garden with a family of tortoises who glide through the greenery. The garden has the same inward-looking coolness it always had, with a Moorish tiled fountain at its center.

cooling off

Not all of us have the resources to install a swimming pool, or even a fountain in the garden, but the sound of running water is always reviving and cooling on a hot summer's day. Fitting an outdoor shower isn't expensive, and is the perfect way to cool down and feel refreshed when the heat gets unbearable. Use utilitarian features like a big shower head and copper pipes, and make sure that water can drain away easily.

left: In a secluded corner, reclaimed and weatherworn timber has been used for a rustic-looking shower screen, and a piece of driftwood forms a shelf for soap and a collection of shells.

right: A decorative seashore garland has been hung from a nail in the shower, adding touches of blue and white to the gray of the wood. Lengths of jute string have been threaded with shells, blue glass, and white ceramic beads, and tied onto a metal ring covered in raffia.

tiled floors

Although the Romans produced beautiful mosaic floors using marble and stone, the first tiled floors were made from simple red terra cotta, or baked clay. It wasn't until after 700 AD, when the influence of Islamic tiling spread from Syria through to Morocco and Spain, that the art came into its own. The intricate, multi-colored tiling techniques perfected by the Moors have never been improved on, but throughout history tiles have been used for floor decorations, from the two-color tiles of medieval monasteries, to the beautiful encaustic patterns of Victorian England. Using tiles outside is a creative way to bring blue-and-white pattern to the garden, whether it is along a path or under a covered loggia.

above: A vibrant blue-and-white zigzag design has been laid in a courtyard, and continued along a short flight of steps. If you are creating a similar effect yourself, make sure that glazed tiles have a non-slip surface that won't become slippery in wet weather.

far left: Mixing a selection of colored tiles with terra cotta creates an elaborate design made from different elements. The strip of complex zellije mosaic is very expensive to install, so it has been surrounded with simpler tiles laid in many diverse directions.

left above: A floor of all-blue tiles looks rich and sumptuous with its narrow border of tiny triangles. The beauty is all in the way the tiles have been placed—rectangular and square are laid in a creative, geometric design.

right: A simple, but effective design for a covered loggia has been achieved with diagonally-laid tiles in blue, green, and white with a herringbone border. The Victorians made similar paths, and reproduction unglazed geometric tiles are a good way to accomplish the same look.

left: A Victorian pine dresser top was riddled with woodworm and in dire need of restoration. But once mended and painted in soft sky blue with a white trim and hung on a landing wall, it is transformed into the perfect display unit for a collection of vintage photograph frames and bottles.

right: Old glass scent bottles with silver tops were made in all sizes. Collected over the years and placed on pale blue shelves, the silver and glass glint in the light and are seen at their best.

collections

Who hasn't felt the thrill of searching through the recesses of an antique market, or scouring tables at a junk sale to triumphantly come across another piece of treasure to add to your collection? Whether it's a blue glass bottle, a Wedgwood jug, a traditional blue-and-white plate, or an enamel storage jar, the secret of any collection is all in the display.

above: A set of matching, tall-stemmed blue wine glasses are brought out for a special occasion dinner party. Unusual glasses like these need to be searched for and kept for best, but they transform any table setting into something out of the ordinary.

above: The simplest displays can often be the most effective. In a Moroccan kitchen, the wall unit was finished using the traditional tadelekt polished plaster technique. Lit from above, a set of modern blue glass tumblers that are used every day are shown off to their best advantage in the niche.

above: The combination of cobalt oxide and lead crystal gives a remarkable deep blue glass, and the English port of Bristol was one of the most important glass-making centers in Europe from 1800 onward. Many bottles were used to hold poison, with "Not to be taken" molded on the side. Crowded together on a kitchen shelf, the blue shows a remarkable depth of color.

left: Willow Pattern china was designed by Thomas Minton in 1770 in response to the passion for all things Chinese. The classic design features an ancient story—a young couple flee an irate father, only to be killed when their hut is set alight, but their spirits turn into doves and fly away.

below: There are as many designs of blue-and-white plates as there are potteries, and china manufactured by Wedgwood, Doulton, and Spode, as well as by a host of lesser-known makers, has always been extremely collectable. Hung against a red brick wall, the stunning cobalt blue glaze of this eclectic collection looks startlingly effective.

right: A ceramic stall in the heart of the Marrakech souk sells mountains of blue-and-white china, mostly made in Fez, which is a center for the manufacture of china decorated with a blue glaze. Striped plates are piled high, and are a simple, contemporary design.

below: In the Villa Maroc, large quantities of china, used every day for serving delicious, traditional Moroccan food, are stacked in an old wooden chest in the hallway instead of being hidden away in cabinets. It's a decorative and innovative way to combine storage and display.

right: In ancient China, covered jars were used for provisions such as oil, salt, and ginger, and were often given as wedding presents. The ubiquitous "ginger jar" is a classic design still being made today, like this modern version decorated with botanical drawings in blue on a white ground.

below: Josiah Spode was a pioneer in his field, and in 1784 he perfected a technique for transfer printing onto earthenware using engraved copper plates. His Blue Italian ware has been made continuously ever since, and has become one of the most collectable ranges in history.

left: After years of experimentation by its founder Josiah Wedgwood, Jasperware, a unique blue stoneware with white bas-relief decorations, was finally unveiled in 1775. Colored with metalic oxides, Jasperware is usually found in pale blue, but other colors, like this deep blue pitcher made in 1900, can also be discovered.

right: Willow Pattern can be found in many different shades of blue, and even in browns and blacks, but the most common is this beautiful deep cobalt blue that was used for the earliest pieces.

left: Mixing styles and periods can make a fascinating and decorative display. On a dining room dresser, a collection of 1940s pastel-colored pitchers sits cheek by jowl with an assorted set of pressed glass and a grouping of Victorian china cake plates decorated with roses.

right: An unusual pairing of two diverse collections allows each to be highlighted by the other. The soft colors of the paintings with their domestic subjects are in total harmony with the natural shapes and materials of the hand-turned wooden and ceramic bowls.

right: These tiles, made by Minton Hollins in about 1880, were reclaimed from a Victorian washstand, and their blue-and-white motifs with classic designs of birds, windmill, and rider on horseback are influenced by the earlier Delftware tiles.

below: In the late Victorian era, the lily was a popular decorative motif used in the design of fabrics, ceramics, jewelry, and lamps. Wall tiles ornamented with the lily would have been used on fireplaces and sideboards, as well as on walls in pantries and kitchens.

right: As early as the sixteenth century, Dutch potters in Delft were making tiles with a white tin glaze that mimicked the white of Chinese porcelain. Typical blue-and-white Delftware is decorated with distinctively vivid hand-painted motifs ranging from small buildings and ships to animals and flowers, like these early tiles made in 1710.

COFFEE   TEA   RICE   SUGAR

above: Enamelware storage jars were very popular in the 1930s and 40s and it is still possible to find plenty of them in junk shops and charity stores, although prices are rising. As any collector of enamelware will verify, the best thing about vintage kitchenalia is using it every day.

left: Blue is a very common color for old enamelware, and dishes and jars can be put to many uses in the kitchen. On a seaside kitchen worktop, this blue container with wooden handles is employed for holding a collection of driftwood and shells as they are brought in from the beach.

right: Often found in French brocante (bric-a-brac) shops and antique markets, enamel pitchers were originally used for carrying hot water in the days before modern plumbing. Far removed from high-class antiques, these utilitarian and serviceable household goods have a rustic charm that makes them very collectable.

below: Ribbons, trims, and braids are always useful for embellishing pillows or lampshades, so it's worth looking out for favorites when you're out on a shopping trip. Buy them whenever you see them and keep them all together in a work basket.

above: Pillows piled on a sofa or bed will bring an instant touch of blue and white to any room. Mixing florals and stripes is a classic combination that works every time and is just as effective in a simple country house or a classic, sophisticated interior.

below: Even if you're not too skilled with the sewing machine, there are plenty of easy projects to make for your home. A pillow will only need a short length of fabric, so it's the perfect opportunity to riffle through a remnant box and pick out three or four different designs. Even a crisp new dish towel can be made into a seat pad or pair of napkins.

above: Vintage table linen must be snapped up when you find it, so amassing a collection of hand-woven napkins and tablecloths might take years. Keep it well-laundered and pressed and bring it out for special occasions.

below: Even damaged china containers can be put to good use if they are planted with hyacinth bulbs for winter flowering. Plant in the early autumn in bulb potting mix and add a little water. Keep in a cool, dark place until the shoots are a couple of inches high, then bring into a warm room and keep moist until they flower.

above: Collections of containers or pitchers can be purely decorative and make wonderful displays, but it's lovely to use them for simple posies of flowers. A blue-and-white jug from the Portmeirion Botanic Blue collection holds a handful of muscari, or grape hyacinths, picked from a spring garden.

below: In winter, hyacinths are one of the few cut flowers that don't look forced or unnatural. Buy a few stems and pack them tightly into a square glass vase for an effortless arrangement that is both stylish and unpretentious.

above: A vintage white enamel pitcher is chipped and stained, and you might draw the line at using it for milk. But spilling over with blue anemones, it makes a pretty and unassuming vase for a country scheme.

useful contacts

Adirondack chairs
Dekkers and Darling
www.dekkersanddarling.com

Allover quilting services
Ferret Fabrications
www.ferfab.co.uk

Riverside Quilting
www.riversidequilting.com

American shutters
The New England Shutter Co
www.thenewenglandshutter company.co.uk

The Plantation Shutter
www.theplantationshutter.com

Antique ginger jars
Dynasty Antiques
www.dynastyantiques.com

Country and Eastern
www.countryandeastern.co.uk

Antique tiles, ceramics, and jewelry
The Hive
www.hiveantiques.co.uk

Blue and white china
The Crockery Barn
www.thecrockerybarn.co.uk

Spode
www.spode.co.uk

Portmeirion
www.portmeirion.co.uk

Blue glass
Bristol Blue Glass
www.bristol-glass.co.uk
www.bristolblueglass.com

Encaustic and geometric tiles
Tiled Pefection
www.tiledperfection.com

The Antique Floor Company
www.theantiquefloorcompany.com

Olde English Tiles
www.oldeenglishtiles.com.au
www.oldeenglishtilesUSA.com

Fabrics
Vanessa Arbuthnott
www.vanessaarbuthnott.co.uk
www.lucyrosedesign.com

Ian Mankin
www.ianmankin.com

Laura Ashley
www.lauraashley.com

Sasha Waddell
www.sashawaddell.co.uk

Malabar
www.malabar.co.uk

Sanderson
www.sanderson-uk.com

Glass mosaic tiles
Fired Earth
www.firedearth.com

Original Style
www.originalstyle.com

Home accessories
Sandra Jane
www.sjah.co.uk
Lombok
www.lombok.co.uk

Laura Ashley
www.lauraashley.com

Froggatt & Frost, Cape Town
www.froggattandfrost.co.za

Khaya Bella, Cape Town
www.khayabella.co.uk

Biggie Best
www.biggiebest.com

Mr Price
www.mrphome.com

Moroccan accessories and ceramics
Moroccan Bazaar
www.moroccanbazaar.co.uk

Just Morocco
www.justmorocco.com

Mosaic
www.e-mosaik.com

New Delftware tiles
Terra Firma Tiles
www.terrafirmatiles.co.uk

Nelis' Dutch Village
www.bluedelft.com

Paint
Farrow & Ball
www.farrow-ball.com

The Little Greene Paint Company
www.littlegreene.com

Kevin McCloud Paint
www.firedearth.com/paint

Reclaimed roll-top baths
Cunningham Lumber
www.cunninghamlumber.com

Seaside accessories
Buy The Sea
www.buythesea.co.uk

Not on the High Street.Com
www.notonthehighstreet.com

Crate and Barrel
www.crateandbarrel.com

Stair runners
Roger Oates
www.rogeroates.com

Laura Ashley
www.lauraashley.com

Stone and composite stone baths
Stonell
www.stonell.com

Apaiser
www.apaiser.com

Tadelakt
Mike Wye & Associates
www.mikewye.co.uk

Artesano LLC
www.artesano-home.com

Teak garden furniture
Barlow Tyrie Ltd
www.teak.com

Towels and bed linen
Pretty Practicals
www.pretty-practicals.com
Christy
www.christy-towels.com

Linum at Cool Calm Collected
www.coolcalmcollected.net

Vintage and monogrammed linen
Parna
www.parna.co.uk

Cherry Valley Antiques
www.cherryvalleyantiques.ca

Vintage enamelware
The Hive
www.hiveantiques.co.uk

Antique Mystique
www.antiquemystique.com

Wallpaper
Farrow & Ball
www.farrow-ball.com

Cole & Son
www.cole-and-son.com

Laura Ashley
www.lauraashley.com

Wedgwood Jasperware
Wedgwood
www.wedgwood.co.uk

Willow Pattern China
Louis Potts
www.louispotts.com

Willow Pattern Collectors Club
www.willowcollectors.org

Blue and White
www.blueandwhite.com

Wrought iron garden furniture
PJH Designs
www.pjhgardenfurniture.com

Places to visit in Marakech
Majorelle Gardens: tropical gardens with Majorelle blue walls and pots.

Museum of Islamic Art, Avenue Yacoub El-Mansour, Marrakech (no phone)

Ben Youssef Medersa: for a good example of zelije tiling, stucco, and carved cedar decoration
Place Ben Youssef, Marrakech
024 39 09 11

Bahia Palace: paved courtyards, arcades, and pavilions decorated with zelije tiling and sculpted stucco
Riad Zitoun, El-Jedid 024 38 92 21

Places to stay in Morocco
The House of Wonders
www.houseofwonders.com

The Best of Morocco
www.morocco-travel.com

Villa Maroc
www.villa-maroc.com

Places to stay in Cape Town
Amazing Spaces
www.amazingspaces.co.za

index

acknowledgments

There are so many people I would like to thank for all their kindness and hard work in helping me to get this book together. From Cambridgeshire to Morocco, East Sussex to South Africa, I met only helpfulness and cooperation. So many thanks everyone.

To Mark Scott, for his truly gifted photography which is always an inspiration, thank you for driving me everywhere in Cape Town, and for introducing me to the city and its wonders, especially the penguins and baboons!

To Gillian Haslam, my editor, for her constant support; to Christine Wood for her inspirational design; to Sally Powell, Art Director, for her picture guidance, and to Cindy Richards for her faith in me.

To Ronald Pile, without whose brilliant French the experience of location hunting in Marrakech would have been very different.

To all those in Morocco who gave us hospitality and advice and opened up their wonderfully chic riads and hotels, and to all at The Best of Morocco and The House of Wonders for their introductions to Villa Maroc, Riad Edward, Les Deux Tours, Caravanserai, Dar Zaouia, Riad Enija and Dar Hani. Also thanks to Riad Edward for looking after us and to our driver Hussein for patiently guiding us around Marrakech.